THE DYNAMITE ADVENTURES OF
DREW SKETCHER

CHARLES WILLIAMS

Copyright © 2018 Charles Williams

All rights reserved. No part of this publication may be reproduced, distributed, or transmitted in any form or by any means, including photocopying, recording, or other electronic methods, without the prior written permission of the publisher, except in the case of brief quotations embodied in critical reviews and certain other noncommercial uses permitted by copyright law.

ISBN: 978-1-945532-54-2

Published by:
Opportune Independent Publishing Company

Printed in the United States of America

For permission requests, write to the publisher, addressed "Attention: Permissions Coordinator," at the address below.

info@opportunepublishing.com
www.opportunepublishing.com

To purchase this book in bulk, or for special orders, visit:
www.drewsketcher.com.

BOOK ONE

Welcome to the Dynamite Adventures of Drew Sketcher, a tale about a boy whose world was turned upside down due to an unexpected special gift. Many great tales lie ahead that includes a universe full of superheroes, outstanding sidekicks, monsters, and many other adventures, all brought to life by Drew. But in order to start any tale, the story must start with...

Once upon a time, there was a young boy by the name of Drew Sketcher. Drew looks and acts like every kid his age. He plays video games, watches cartoons, draws, and, of course, hates eating vegetables. But Drew will soon come to realize that he has one special gift that makes him unique to all the other kids. But in order to see this special gift, we must first follow Drew as he embarks on his daily adventure. Why, here is Drew now sound asleep in his bedroom. Looks like the sun is starting to sneak into his bedroom, so that means we are just in time for...

Buzz! Buzz! Buzz! The sound of Drew's alarm clock goes off. Ugh! Drew tosses and turns in his bed trying to sleep over the loud noise of his alarm clock. The alarm continues Buzz! Buzz! Buzz! Suddenly, the bedroom door opens; it's Drew's mother coming in to make sure he wakes up to get ready for school. A bright light instantly fills the room as she flips the light switch. Drew's mother says, "Drew... Drew, it's time sweetie, come on wake up and go brush your teeth."

Drew lets out a light moan and he slides his head under the bedsheets as a last attempt to remain in his dream world. Drew pleads with his mother, "Mommy, I don't feel good. My throat hurts (cough), I think I'm sick, mommy."

She replies, "Come on Drew, you use this excuse every morning. Time to get up, come on." His mother pulls the bedsheets from over his body, instantly waking him as the cool air touches his once-warm body.

After the daily fuss over the morning wake-up call, Drew is finally dressed and on the road heading to school. Inside the car, Drew's mother says, "So Drew, how has school been so far? Have you made any new friends yet?"

Drew replies, "Not really mommy."

"Well, sweetie, I remember when I was around your age I had to move to a new school too. It took time for me to make new friends myself."

Drew looks at his feet and says, "There is this kid at school that calls me mean names."

Drew's mother raises her voice, "What?! What is his name Drew?"

Drew replies, "His name is Jacob and he picks on me every day."

Drew's mother says, "Well don't you worry about Jacob anymore, Drew, I'll talk to the school about this."

Drew's mother pulls up to the front of the school. After giving his mother a hug, Drew reaches to open the car door. Right before Drew pulls the handle his mother says, "Hold on a second sweetie, I know it's two days before your birthday but I think you should have this today. Maybe this will cheer you up."

Drew's mother grabs her bag from the back seat and pulls out a present. Excited, Drew tears open the wrapper to reveal a sketchbook, art supplies, and a messenger bag. Drew shouts, "Wow, Mom! This looks just like the bag daddy uses for work."

She replies, "Your father and I felt this would be perfect for you, with you moving to a new city and always trying to use his old briefcases."

Drew gives his mother one more big hug, squeezing as tight as his can, and says, "Thanks, Mommy!"

He grabs his gifts, opens the car door, and heads to his school.

Later on that day Drew is with his father, in his home office, drawing on his new sketchbook. Drew's dad walks by and notices his drawings. Then he asks, "What is that you are drawing, champ?"

Drew replies, "It's a superhero, daddy."

Drew's dad leans over the table to look at his drawings "Oh really," he says to Drew "Let me take a look at that."

Drew slides his sketchbook over to his father. Drew's dad points at one of his drawings and says, "He kind of looks like you, Drew. Do you have a name for him?"

Drew replies, "Um, no, I don't, dad. Can you help me name him?"

His dad asks Drew, "Well what are his powers Drew?"

Drew answers, "He can freeze things and create ice shields. He can also… Umm… He can also create ice walls and he helps his city with arresting bad guys."

Drew's dad thinks for a second then begins to smile. "I got it!" Drew's dad shouts, "We can name him 40 Below."

Drew looks at his dad with a curious look on his face. His dad continues, "It's because he can freeze things and 40 Below is very, very cold, Drew."

Drew shouts, "That's an awesome name!" Drew's father notices another drawing and asks, "Oh, who is that right beside him?"

Drew replies, "Oh, that is his sidekick, Inspector Paws."

Drew's father burst out in laughter. "Drew, Inspector Paws almost looks our cat like Mittens," said Drew's dad.

Drew replies, "He is Mittens daddy. He helps 40 Below to stop mean people from doing bad things."

Drew's dad begins to settle down with his laughter and says, "Sounds really cool Drew, do you have anyone else?"

Drew slides his sketchbook over and shows another drawing to his dad. His father asks, "Who is that?"

Drew says, "That is Jacob and he is one of the bad guys that 40 Below and Inspector Paws must stop from doing bad things. I don't have a name for him either." Drew's dad says, "Your mother told me about this Jacob kid. Don't worry, Drew, your mother will handle everything."

Drew's dad takes a long look at the drawing of the character. He notices it's a man wearing a leather vest and denim jeans. Everything looks normal except one detail; he has the head of a bull. Drew's dad says, "Hmm... So you need help with naming him too, Drew?"

Drew answers, "Yes please."

Drew's dad replies, "How about we call him T-Bone since he has a bull's head."

Drew and his father share a laugh and continue to talk as time passes along. Drew's dad

looks at his watch and says, "Oh wow, it's past your bedtime, Drew. Come on, let's get you upstairs and ready for bed before mommy makes us both go to bed."

Drew is sound asleep in his bed when suddenly he wakes up to faint noise in his bedroom. Whomp! Whomp! Whomp! Whomp! Drew opens his eyes to see that his sketchbook is lighting up and making noise. Drew slowly walks over to his sketchbook; his hand starts to move towards the front cover. Drew opens his sketchbook. Then the room instantly filled with a blinding light. Drew feels himself being pulled into his sketchbook.

Drew hears a faint voice slowly increase in volume,

"Hello... Hello... HEY, 40 Below! Wake up! Hey!"

SPLASH! Drew is hit with a bucket of water which causes him to instantly open his eyes. Drew, now confused, asks, "Woah! What? What just happened?"

The voice responds, "Hey 40 B! Wake up, sleepy head. Geez, and I thought I slept a lot through the day."

Drew's vision begins to focus in and he notices the voice is coming from a cat holding a magnifying glass. Drew jumps up and screams, "WHOA! Who are you? Where am I? Where is my room?"

The cat answers, "40 B, what are you talking about? You are at the office and fell asleep."

Drew now begins to notice that the cat looks very familiar. Drew says, "Wait, is that ... Is that you, Mittens?"

The cat answers, "Whoa, buddy, I don't know who this Mittens fella is. 40 B it's me, Inspector Paws. Come on man, the mayor has been trying to talk to you for hours."

Drew takes a closer look at his surroundings. Drew says, "Wait a minute, am I in my sketchbook?"

Inspector Paws responds, "You're what? We don't have time for this, 40 B, we need to go see the Mayor. It sounded like it was urgent when he called our phone earlier."

Later at the Mayor's Office... "Oh my, this is bad, this is really bad, oh my, oh my," the Mayor said while pacing circles around his office.

"Excuse me, Mayor," said a voice coming from the speaker of the Mayor's office phone.

The Mayor replies, "Yes, what's going on, Ms. Mazuca?"

Ms. Mazuca replies, "Sir 40 Below and Inspector Paws have arrived; would you like for me to send them in?"

The Mayor answers, "Finally! Yes, Ms. Mazuca. Send them in."

40 Below and Inspector Paws enter the Mayor's office. "I'm so glad you two finally made it," the Mayor said.

Inspector Paws says, "What's the skinny, Mayor? Is it Old Man Charlie and Old Lady Dee throwing squirrels at each other again?"

The Mayor says, "No, it's not that, I'm afraid it's much worse. Much, much worse."

40 Below asks, "Well what is the problem, Mayor?"

The Mayor replies, "It's T-Bone. He is loose and he's making a mess of things all around the city."

Inspector Paws shouts, "T-Bone is loose? Oh man! This is pretty bad news."

Inspector Paws jumps out of his chair and says, "Don't worry Mayor, 40 B and I will handle this. You ready, 40 B? It's time to get dangerous."

40 Below and Inspector Paws run out of the Mayor's office to go confront T-Bone. Outside the Mayor's office 40 Below turns to Inspector Paws and asks, "So where do you think we will find T-Bone Inspector Paws?"

Inspector Paws replies, "Hmm... Well, let's take a look around and find out."

Inspector Paws raises his magnifying glass to his eye and begins to scan the outside surroundings.

Inspector Paws says, "Well if T-Bone is destroying things around the city I should be able to see the smoke and fire. Let me switch my lens to pick up on large smoke clouds." Inspector Paws pushes a button on his magnifying glass thereafter, a voice says, "Yes, Inspector?"

Inspector Paws says, "Maggie, focus your lens to pinpoint abnormal amounts smoke."

After a few scans Inspector Paws shouts, "Found it! It looks like there is a huge smoke cloud coming from the town park. Let's hurry so we can stop T-Bone before he causes any more damage."

40 Below and Inspector Paws jump on their crime-cycle to rush over to T-Bone's position. "40 B, you drive and I will navigate," said Inspector Paws.

40 Below sits in the driver's seat. While sitting panic suddenly takes over his body after taking one look at the controls. 40 Below turns to Inspector Paws and says, "Um Inspector Paws, I don't know how to drive."

With a confused look, Inspector Paws replied, "Of course you do, 40 B. What is going on with you today, dude?"

40 Below takes a deep breath, and then says, "Okay put on your seatbelt Inspector Paws, here goes nothing."

40 Below starts the engine of the crime-cycle. He sets the gear to drive then...

SCREECH! "Wait a second, I think I got....Okay, that was not right," said 40 Below.

SCREECH! "Sorry Inspector Paws, but I think I got it now," Said 40 Below.

SCREECH! "Oh geez," cried Inspector Paws. He smacks his palm on his forehead and says, "40 B, never mind I'll drive; just hold Maggie over your eye and tell me where to go."

40 Below replies, "Sorry Inspector Paws."

40 Below and Inspector Paws switch seats, then drive off to go stop T-Bone. The crime-cycle arrives at the town park; it is a scene of utter chaos, all caused by T-Bone. Inspector Paws shouts, "Oh man, 40 B. It's worse than we thought. Quick! We don't have any more time to waste."

While destroying some parker equipment, T-Bone notices 40 Below and Inspector Paws. T-Bone turns his attention towards the two heroes and says, "Well, well. Looks like the two super dorks finally showed up."

Inspector Paws replies, "Okay. We have two choices here, T-Bone. You can come with us peacefully or you can come to us as a beef-flavored popsicle."

T-Bone charged at 40 Below and Inspector Paws. "Well, you asked for the bull, now here comes the horns," cried T-Bone.

40 Below shouts, "Look out!"

WACK! T-Bone rams into 40 Below and Inspector Paws knocking them to the ground. Inspector Paws slowly stands up and says, "Ugh, my head. Hey, 40 B, are you okay?"

40 Below is still laying on his back and does not respond. Inspector Paws tries again but still, 40 Below does not respond. "Dang it. Okay Maggie, looks like it's you and me for right now," said Inspector Paws.

"Maggie, switch to the solar flare," cried Inspector Paws.

Inspector Paws holds his magnifying glass high above his head; the glass begins to glow a bright red as it absorbs the energy from the sun. "Solar flare is fully charged, sir," said Maggie.

Inspector Paws points the magnifying glass towards T-Bone. "I hope you're ready to become a hamburger... Maggie, Fire!" Said Inspector Paws.

A beam of light shoots out of Inspector Paws' magnifying glass heading directly to T-Bone. BOOM! The beam of energy strikes T-Bone, sending him flying back to the monkey bars.

Meanwhile... 40 Below, while lying on the ground, begins to open his eyes. "Ugh my head," said 40 Below.

He slowly sits up. Then, a rush of memories flashes before his eyes. 40 Below shakes his head and whispers, "Wait... I remember everything now."

40 Below stands up and notices Inspector Paws battling T-Bone. T-Bone stands up holding his head. Still partially dazed from Inspector Paws' attack. Enraged T--Bone screams, "RRRROOAAAHHHHHH! I'll clobber the both of you."

T-Bone turns and rips the broken monkey bars out of the ground and crushes them to form a metal ball. "Batter up, dorks," said T-Bone, as he throws the balled-up monkey bars directly at our heroes.

Suddenly, a thick wall of ice forms in front of Inspector Paws, immediately stopping the balled-up monkey bars. Inspector Paws looks over at 40 Below and says, "Whew, good job 40 B, for a second there I thought I was going to have eight lives."

T-Bone begins to charge directly towards Inspector Paws. Inspector Paws leaps in the air, dodging T-Bone's attack. BONK! Inspector Paws strikes T-Bone's head with his magnifying glass, which leaves him dazed. While dazed, 40 Below shoots a beam of ice that completely encases T-Bone in a frozen box. 40 Below walks cautiously towards his partner and asks, "Is ...Is it over, Inspector Paws?"

Inspector Paws answers, "Yeah you turned him into an ice cube. Go call the Mayor to let him know that T-Bone has been stopped."

Later at the Mayor's Office... "The town can't thank you enough, 40 Below and Inspector Paws," said the Mayor.

40 Below responds, "Not a problem, Mayor."

The Mayor continues to talk but 40 Below can no longer hear his voice. Suddenly, the environment around 40 Below begins to turn white. 40 Below says, "What's going...."

Buzz! Buzz! Buzz! The sound of Drew's alarm clock goes off. Drew jumps up and looks over at his sketchbook. The sketchbook is closed and does not seem to have moved and inch. Drew whispers to himself, "Was that a dream?"

The alarm continues, Buzz! Buzz! Buzz! Drew's mother walks into his room and says, "Drew it's time to... Oh, you are awake already."

Drew gets dressed, places his sketchbook in his messenger bag, and is silently staring out the car window during the car ride to school. At one point during the car ride, Drew's mother asks, "Is everything okay with you sweetie?"

Drew turns away from the window and right before he is about to start his answer, a cell phone begins to ring. "Oh, hold on just a second Drew, this is work," said Drew's mother while answering the incoming call.

The car pulls up to the drop off point at his school. Still on the cell phone, Drew's mother says, "Josh... Joshua he... Hey Joshua, hold on a second I have to say bye to my son."

Drew's mother places the phone on her shoulder and turns to tell Drew bye and blows a kiss to him. Drew screams in embarrassment, "Eww! Not in front of my friends' mom."

Laughing at his reaction Drew's mom blows four more kisses. Drew runs into the school hoping to dodge the onslaught of kisses heading towards him.

While walking the hallway to his class Drew notices Jacob heading down the opposite way of the hallway. Suddenly the feeling of fear takes over Drew and at that moment all he can think of is his dream from last night. Drew wants to turn and walk the opposite way but his legs are frozen in place due to fear. Jacob notices Drew and begins to walk towards his direction. More thoughts fill Drew's mind about how 40 Below was brave enough to face T-Bone.

Suddenly Drew remembers, he was 40 Below. Now the feeling of fear turns into a feeling of bravery. Drew whispers to himself, "I got to do this, I have to stand up for myself."

Jacob approaches Drew and says, "Hey Drew, my mom, and dad told me that your mom called them and said I was bullying you. They also told me that if I ever do it again you tell your mom to call them and let them know about it. Hey Drew, I'm really sorry my mom and dad told me about how much I was hurting your feelings."

Drew is absolutely stunned over what is happening and all he can think to say is, "Thank you, Jacob."

Jacob replies, "Can you just let your mom know I said sorry; my mom said she would call your mom to check if I did."

Drew answers, "Okay, I will let her know."

Jacob reaches into his lunch bag and pulls out a candy bar.

"Hey, do you want this candy bar? It can be our peace offering," asked Jacob.

Drew, with a surprised look on his face, replies, "Um, yeah, thanks! Want to come over to my house and play video games after school; well when I am no longer grounded?"

Drew replies, "Okay."

Drew walks to his classroom and sits at his desk. He starts to take items out of his messenger bag. He notices his sketchbook is inside. Still curious about his dream that felt so real to him Drew takes out his sketchbook and flips through the pages. He notices new images that he does not remember drawing on the pages. The new images oddly resemble everything that happened during his dream. Drew continues to flip through the pages until finally reaching the first blank page. Drew flips the page back to reveal the final drawing.

It's a drawing of 40 Below, Inspector Paws, and T-Bone all playing video games and laughing.

Below the drawing, Drew notices a sentence that reads, "The day is saved and now we are all friends."

Drew's eyes open wide after reading the sentence. He quickly closes the sketchbook and whispers to himself, "My sketchbook ... Is it magic?"

www.ingramcontent.com/pod-product-compliance
Lightning Source LLC
Chambersburg PA
CBHW041322110526
44591CB00021B/2878